Crunch & Crust

The Ultimate Toasted Bread Cookbook

CRUNCH & CRUST

First edition. March 3, 2024.

ISBN: 979-8224534104

Written by Jose Maria.

Table of Contents

Jose Maria

❖ Introduction: The Art of Toasting

Toasting bread has been a culinary tradition spanning cultures and centuries, transforming simple slices of bread into flavorful delights. This introductory chapter delves into the rich history and significance of toasted bread in culinary traditions around the world, highlighting its evolution from a practical means of preserving bread to a beloved culinary technique cherished for its taste and texture.

Origins of Toasting Bread

The act of toasting bread dates back to ancient civilizations, where it served as a method of preserving bread and revitalizing stale loaves. Early civilizations, including the Egyptians and Romans, toasted bread over open flames or hot stones to remove moisture and extend its shelf life. This simple preservation technique evolved over time, with various cultures incorporating toasted bread into their culinary practices.

Culinary Significance

Beyond its practical origins, toasted bread holds a special place in culinary traditions worldwide. It provides a canvas for a myriad of flavors and textures, serving as a versatile base for both savory and sweet creations. Whether enjoyed as a simple breakfast staple or elevated to gourmet status in elaborate dishes, toasted bread embodies comfort, nostalgia, and innovation in the kitchen.

Toasting Techniques

Toasting bread is an art form that requires attention to detail and an understanding of various techniques to achieve optimal results. This section serves as a comprehensive guide to mastering the art of toasting, exploring different methods and their respective outcomes.

Methods of Toasting Bread

1. Toaster: The most common method of toasting bread, utilizing

an electric toaster to evenly brown slices to desired crispiness.

2. Oven: Toasting bread in the oven allows for larger quantities to be toasted at once, with the option to customize the level of browning by adjusting the temperature and broil settings.

3. Stovetop: Toasting bread on a stovetop skillet or griddle offers precise control over the toasting process, allowing for even browning and the option to add butter or oil for extra flavor.

4. Open Flame: For a rustic touch, bread can be toasted over an open flame, imparting a smoky flavor and charred edges reminiscent of outdoor cooking methods.

5. Grill: Grilling bread over hot coals or a gas grill adds a delightful smokiness and grill marks, perfect for outdoor gatherings and barbecues.

Conclusion

The art of toasting bread transcends mere culinary technique, embodying centuries of tradition, innovation, and creativity. From its humble origins as a means of preservation to its revered status in modern cuisine, toasted bread continues to inspire chefs and home cooks alike to explore its endless possibilities. In the following chapters, we'll delve deeper into the world of toasted bread, exploring classic creations, gourmet sandwiches, creative delights, international treats, and sweet endings. Join us on a journey to discover the boundless potential of this humble yet versatile culinary staple.

Chapter 1: Classic Toast Creations

1. Basic Toast:
Ingredients:

- Slices of your favorite bread (white, whole wheat, sourdough, etc.)

Instructions:

- Place your bread slices into a toaster or toaster oven.
- Adjust the settings to your desired level of toastiness.
- Toast the bread until it reaches a perfect golden brown color and a satisfying crunch.
- Remove the toasted bread slices from the toaster and transfer them to a plate.
- Serve hot and customize with your favorite toppings, such as butter, jam, honey, avocado, peanut butter, or cream cheese.

2. French Toast:
Ingredients:

- Thick slices of bread (such as brioche or challah)
- 2 large eggs
- 1/2 cup milk
- 1 teaspoon vanilla extract
- 1/2 teaspoon ground cinnamon
- Butter or oil for cooking
- Maple syrup, powdered sugar, fresh fruit (optional, for serving)

Instructions:

1. In a shallow bowl, whisk together eggs, milk, vanilla extract, and

ground cinnamon until well combined.

2. Heat a skillet or griddle over medium heat and add a knob of butter or a drizzle of oil.
3. Dip each slice of bread into the egg mixture, allowing it to soak for a few seconds on each side.
4. Place the soaked bread slices onto the hot skillet or griddle and cook until golden brown and crispy on both sides, about 2-3 minutes per side.
5. Once cooked, transfer the French toast to a serving plate.
6. Serve hot with maple syrup, a dusting of powdered sugar, and fresh fruit if desired.

3. Garlic Bread:
Ingredients:

- Sliced French or Italian bread loaf
- 1/2 cup unsalted butter, softened
- 2 cloves garlic, minced
- 2 tablespoons fresh parsley, finely chopped
- Salt and pepper to taste

Instructions:

1. Preheat the oven to 375°F (190°C).
2. In a small bowl, mix together softened butter, minced garlic, chopped parsley, salt, and pepper until well combined.
3. Slice the bread loaf in half lengthwise and place it on a baking sheet, cut side up.
4. Spread the garlic butter mixture evenly over the cut sides of the bread loaf.
5. Bake in the preheated oven for 10-12 minutes, or until the bread is crispy and golden brown around the edges.
6. Remove from the oven and let it cool for a few minutes before

slicing.

7. Slice the garlic bread into individual portions and serve warm as a flavorful accompaniment to pasta, soup, or salad.

4. Bruschetta:
Ingredients:

- Baguette, sliced into 1/2-inch thick rounds
- 2 ripe tomatoes, diced
- 2 cloves garlic, minced
- 2 tablespoons fresh basil, thinly sliced
- 2 tablespoons extra virgin olive oil
- Salt and pepper to taste

Instructions:

1. Preheat the oven to 375°F (190°C).
2. Place the baguette slices on a baking sheet and toast them in the preheated oven for 5-7 minutes, or until lightly golden and crisp.
3. In a mixing bowl, combine diced tomatoes, minced garlic, sliced basil, extra virgin olive oil, salt, and pepper. Mix well to combine.
4. Remove the toasted baguette slices from the oven and let them cool slightly.
5. Top each toasted baguette slice with a generous spoonful of the tomato mixture.
6. Arrange the bruschetta on a serving platter and drizzle with additional olive oil, if desired.
7. Serve immediately as a delightful appetizer or light snack.

Chapter 2: Gourmet Toasted Sandwiches

1. Grilled Cheese:
Ingredients:

- 4 slices of your favorite bread (sourdough, ciabatta, or multigrain)
- 2 tablespoons unsalted butter, softened
- 1 cup shredded cheese (choose a combination of your favorite artisanal cheeses such as cheddar, Gruyère, or fontina)
- Optional add-ons: sliced tomatoes, caramelized onions, cooked bacon, or avocado slices

Instructions:

1. Heat a skillet or griddle over medium heat.
2. Spread one side of each bread slice with softened butter.
3. Place two bread slices, buttered side down, on the skillet.
4. Sprinkle shredded cheese evenly over the bread slices in the skillet.
5. Add any desired add-ons on top of the cheese.
6. Top each sandwich with the remaining bread slices, buttered side up.
7. Cook until the bottom bread slices are golden brown and crispy, and the cheese starts to melt, about 3-4 minutes.
8. Carefully flip the sandwiches and continue cooking until the other side is golden brown and the cheese is fully melted, about 3-4 minutes more.
9. Remove from the skillet and let cool slightly before slicing.
10. Serve hot and enjoy the gooey, cheesy goodness of this elevated classic.

2. Avocado Toast:

Ingredients:

- 2 slices of your favorite bread (sourdough, whole grain, or rye)
- 1 ripe avocado
- Salt and pepper to taste
- Optional toppings: sliced cherry tomatoes, crumbled feta cheese, red pepper flakes, or poached eggs

Instructions:

1. Toast the bread slices until golden brown and crispy.
2. While the bread is toasting, halve the avocado, remove the pit, and scoop the flesh into a small bowl.
3. Mash the avocado with a fork until smooth and creamy.
4. Season the mashed avocado with salt and pepper to taste, and mix well.
5. Once the bread slices are toasted, spread the mashed avocado evenly over each slice.
6. Top the avocado toast with your desired toppings, such as sliced cherry tomatoes, crumbled feta cheese, or a sprinkle of red pepper flakes.
7. Serve immediately and enjoy this trendy and nutritious treat for breakfast, brunch, or a light meal.

3. Croque Monsieur/Madame:
Ingredients:

- 4 slices of thick-cut bread (such as brioche or country white)
- 4 slices of cooked ham
- 1 cup shredded Gruyère cheese
- 2 tablespoons unsalted butter
- 2 tablespoons all-purpose flour
- 1 cup whole milk
- 1/4 teaspoon ground nutmeg

- Salt and pepper to taste
- Optional: Dijon mustard for Croque Monsieur, fried or poached egg for Croque Madame

Instructions:

1. Preheat the oven to 375°F (190°C).
2. Place 2 slices of bread on a baking sheet and top each with a slice of cooked ham.
3. Sprinkle shredded Gruyère cheese evenly over the ham.
4. Place the remaining bread slices on top to make sandwiches.
5. In a small saucepan, melt the butter over medium heat.
6. Stir in the flour and cook for 1-2 minutes to make a roux.
7. Gradually whisk in the milk, nutmeg, salt, and pepper, and cook until the sauce thickens, about 5 minutes.
8. Pour the sauce over the sandwiches, making sure they are fully coated.
9. Sprinkle additional shredded Gruyère cheese on top of each sandwich.
10. Bake in the preheated oven for 10-12 minutes, or until the sandwiches are golden brown and the cheese is bubbly and melted.
11. For Croque Madame, fry or poach eggs to your desired doneness and place one on top of each sandwich before serving.
12. Serve hot and indulge in the indulgent flavors of these gourmet ham and cheese sandwiches.

4. Panini Varieties:

Ingredients:

- Your choice of bread (ciabatta, focaccia, or baguette), sliced horizontally

- Assorted fillings such as sliced deli meats (turkey, ham, roast beef), cheeses (mozzarella, provolone, Swiss), vegetables (roasted peppers, caramelized onions, spinach), and spreads (pesto, aioli, mustard)

Instructions:

1. Preheat a panini press or grill pan over medium heat.
2. Assemble your sandwiches by layering your chosen fillings between the slices of bread.
3. Spread a thin layer of butter or olive oil on the outside of the sandwiches to help them crisp up and prevent sticking to the panini press or grill pan.
4. Place the assembled sandwiches onto the preheated panini press or grill pan.
5. Close the panini press or cover the sandwiches with a heavy lid in the grill pan to press them down.
6. Cook the sandwiches for 3-4 minutes on each side, or until the bread is golden brown and the fillings are heated through and cheese is melted.
7. Carefully remove the sandwiches from the panini press or grill pan and let them cool for a minute before slicing.
8. Serve hot and enjoy these pressed sandwiches filled with gourmet ingredients and spreads for a delicious and satisfying meal.

Chapter 3: Creative Toasted Delights

1. Breakfast Toast Bowls:
   Ingredients:

- Thick slices of bread (such as country loaf or sourdough)
- Eggs
- Milk
- Salt and pepper to taste
- Assorted vegetables (bell peppers, onions, spinach, tomatoes, etc.)
- Grated cheese (cheddar, mozzarella, feta, etc.)
- Fresh herbs (parsley, chives, basil, etc.)

Instructions:

1. Preheat the oven to 375°F (190°C).
2. Cut the top off each slice of bread and hollow out the center to create a bowl shape, leaving about 1/2 inch of bread around the edges.
3. In a bowl, whisk together eggs, milk, salt, and pepper to make scrambled eggs.
4. Heat a skillet over medium heat and add a bit of oil or butter. Sauté the vegetables until they are tender.
5. Pour the scrambled egg mixture into the skillet with the vegetables and cook until the eggs are set.
6. Fill each bread bowl with the scrambled egg and vegetable mixture.
7. Top each toast bowl with grated cheese and fresh herbs.
8. Place the filled bread bowls on a baking sheet and bake in the preheated oven for about 10-12 minutes, or until the cheese is melted and bubbly.

9. Serve hot and enjoy these hearty and delicious breakfast toast bowls.

2. Stuffed Toast Rolls:
Ingredients:

- Slices of bread (white, wheat, or whole grain)
- Sweet fillings (nutella, peanut butter, jam, honey, etc.)
- Savory fillings (sliced deli meats, cheese, avocado, lettuce, etc.)

Instructions:

1. Flatten each slice of bread using a rolling pin to make it easier to roll.
2. Spread your desired sweet or savory filling evenly over the surface of the bread slice.
3. Roll up the bread slice tightly, starting from one end and rolling towards the other end.
4. If desired, secure the roll with toothpicks to prevent it from unraveling.
5. Heat a skillet over medium heat and add a bit of butter or oil.
6. Place the stuffed toast rolls in the skillet and cook until they are golden brown and crispy on all sides, turning occasionally.
7. Once cooked, remove the stuffed toast rolls from the skillet and let them cool slightly before serving.
8. Serve warm and enjoy these portable and customizable snacks.

3. Toasted Bread Pizzas:
Ingredients:

- Slices of bread (baguette, Italian bread, or ciabatta)
- Pizza sauce
- Shredded mozzarella cheese
- Assorted pizza toppings (pepperoni, bell peppers, mushrooms,

onions, olives, etc.)

- Italian seasoning or dried herbs (basil, oregano, thyme, etc.)

Instructions:

1. Preheat the oven to 375°F (190°C).
2. Place the slices of bread on a baking sheet lined with parchment paper.
3. Spread a thin layer of pizza sauce over each slice of bread.
4. Sprinkle shredded mozzarella cheese evenly over the sauce.
5. Arrange your desired pizza toppings on top of the cheese.
6. Sprinkle Italian seasoning or dried herbs over the toppings.
7. Bake in the preheated oven for about 10-12 minutes, or until the cheese is melted and bubbly and the edges of the bread are golden brown.
8. Remove from the oven and let cool for a minute before serving.
9. Serve hot and enjoy these quick and easy personal pizzas.

4. Toasted Bread Pudding:
Ingredients:

- Slices of bread (brioche, challah, or French bread), cubed
- Eggs
- Milk or heavy cream
- Sugar
- Vanilla extract
- Cinnamon
- Optional sweet additions (raisins, chocolate chips, nuts, etc.)

Instructions:

1. Preheat the oven to 350°F (175°C).
2. Grease a baking dish with butter or cooking spray.
3. In a large bowl, whisk together eggs, milk or heavy cream, sugar,

vanilla extract, and cinnamon until well combined.

4. Add the cubed bread slices to the egg mixture and toss to coat evenly. Let the bread soak for about 10-15 minutes.

5. If desired, stir in any optional sweet additions such as raisins, chocolate chips, or nuts.

6. Pour the bread mixture into the prepared baking dish and spread it out evenly.

7. Bake in the preheated oven for about 35-40 minutes, or until the bread pudding is set and golden brown on top.

8. Remove from the oven and let cool for a few minutes before serving.

9. Serve warm with a drizzle of caramel sauce, whipped cream, or ice cream if desired.

10. Enjoy this comforting and delicious dessert made with toasted bread.

Chapter 4: International Toasted Treats

1. Crostini:
Ingredients:

- Baguette or Italian bread, sliced into thin rounds
- Olive oil
- Toppings:
- Tomato and basil
- Mozzarella and pesto
- Ricotta and honey
- Prosciutto and fig
- Goat cheese and roasted red pepper

Instructions:

1. Preheat the oven to 375°F (190°C).
2. Place the bread slices on a baking sheet and brush lightly with olive oil on both sides.
3. Bake in the preheated oven for 8-10 minutes, or until golden brown and crispy.
4. Remove from the oven and let cool slightly.
5. Top each toasted bread slice with your choice of toppings.
6. Serve immediately as an appetizer or snack.

2. Spanish Pan con Tomate:
Ingredients:

- Slices of rustic bread (such as country loaf or sourdough)
- Ripe tomatoes, halved
- Garlic cloves, peeled
- Extra virgin olive oil
- Sea salt

Instructions:

1. Toast the bread slices until golden brown and crispy.
2. Rub each toasted bread slice with the cut side of a halved tomato, squeezing to release the juices and pulp onto the bread.
3. Rub a peeled garlic clove over the tomato-rubbed bread to infuse it with garlic flavor.
4. Drizzle extra virgin olive oil over the bread and sprinkle with sea salt to taste.
5. Serve immediately as a simple and delicious snack or appetizer.

3. Mexican Molletes:

Ingredients:

- Bolillo rolls or sliced French bread
- Refried beans
- Shredded cheese (queso fresco, Monterey Jack, or cheddar)
- Salsa (store-bought or homemade)
- Optional toppings: sliced avocado, chopped cilantro, diced onions, sliced jalapeños

Instructions:

1. Preheat the oven to 375°F (190°C).
2. Slice the bolillo rolls in half lengthwise and place them cut side up on a baking sheet.
3. Spread a generous layer of refried beans on each bolillo half.
4. Sprinkle shredded cheese over the beans.
5. Bake in the preheated oven for 8-10 minutes, or until the cheese is melted and bubbly.
6. Remove from the oven and top each mollete with salsa and your desired toppings.
7. Serve hot as a delicious and hearty snack or light meal.

4. Scandinavian Smørrebrød:
Ingredients:

- Slices of dense rye bread or pumpernickel bread
- Butter or mayonnaise
- Assorted toppings:
- Smoked salmon, cucumber, and dill
- Pickled herring, red onion, and boiled egg
- Roast beef, horseradish cream, and crispy onions
- Egg salad, radishes, and watercress

Instructions:

1. Spread a thin layer of butter or mayonnaise on each slice of bread.
2. Arrange your chosen toppings on top of the buttered bread slices.
3. Serve immediately as an open-faced sandwich, traditionally enjoyed with a fork and knife.
4. These international toasted treats offer a delightful variety of flavors and textures, perfect for entertaining or simply enjoying as a flavorful snack.

Chapter 5: Sweet Endings with Toasted Bread

1. Cinnamon Toast:
  Ingredients:

- Slices of bread (white, wheat, or sourdough)
- Butter, softened
- Cinnamon sugar (mix cinnamon powder with granulated sugar)

Instructions:

1. Preheat the oven to 375°F (190°C).
2. Spread a thin layer of softened butter over each slice of bread.
3. Sprinkle cinnamon sugar evenly over the buttered bread slices.
4. Place the bread slices on a baking sheet lined with parchment paper.
5. Bake in the preheated oven for 8-10 minutes, or until the bread is golden brown and crispy.
6. Remove from the oven and let cool slightly before serving.
7. Serve warm and enjoy this nostalgic and comforting treat.

2. Bread and Butter Pudding:
Ingredients:

- Slices of bread (brioche, challah, or French bread), toasted and buttered
- Eggs
- Milk
- Sugar
- Vanilla extract
- Cinnamon

- Raisins or other dried fruits (optional)

Instructions:

1. Preheat the oven to 350°F (175°C).
2. Arrange the toasted and buttered bread slices in a greased baking dish, overlapping them slightly.
3. In a bowl, whisk together eggs, milk, sugar, vanilla extract, and cinnamon until well combined.
4. Pour the egg mixture over the bread slices, making sure they are evenly coated.
5. If desired, sprinkle raisins or other dried fruits over the bread pudding.
6. Bake in the preheated oven for 30-35 minutes, or until the custard is set and the top is golden brown.
7. Remove from the oven and let cool for a few minutes before serving.
8. Serve warm with a drizzle of caramel sauce or a dollop of whipped cream if desired.

3. Toasted Bread Ice Cream Sandwiches:
Ingredients:

- Slices of bread (white, wheat, or brioche)
- Ice cream (your favorite flavor)
- Optional add-ons: chocolate chips, crushed nuts, sprinkles

Instructions:

1. Toast the bread slices until golden brown and crispy.
2. Let the toasted bread slices cool completely.
3. Once cooled, spread a scoop of ice cream onto one slice of

bread.

4. Sprinkle any desired add-ons over the ice cream.
5. Top with another slice of toasted bread to form a sandwich.
6. Repeat the process to make additional ice cream sandwiches.
7. Place the ice cream sandwiches in the freezer for at least 30 minutes to firm up.
8. Remove from the freezer and serve cold as a delightful and unique frozen treat.

4. Nutella-Stuffed French Toast:
Ingredients:

- Slices of bread (challah, brioche, or French bread)
- Nutella or chocolate hazelnut spread
- Eggs
- Milk
- Vanilla extract
- Butter, for cooking
- Fresh berries, for topping

Instructions:

1. Spread Nutella or chocolate hazelnut spread onto one side of each slice of bread.
2. Sandwich the bread slices together to form pairs, with the Nutella spread on the inside.
3. In a shallow bowl, whisk together eggs, milk, and vanilla extract until well combined.
4. Dip each stuffed bread sandwich into the egg mixture, coating both sides evenly.
5. Heat a skillet or griddle over medium heat and add a knob of butter.
6. Cook the stuffed bread sandwiches on the skillet until golden

brown and crispy on both sides, flipping once.

7. Once cooked, remove from the skillet and transfer to serving plates.
8. Top with fresh berries and a drizzle of maple syrup or honey.
9. Serve hot and indulge in the decadent flavors of this Nutella-stuffed French toast.

Chapter 6: Healthy Toasted Options

1. Whole Grain Toast with Nut Butter:
Ingredients:

- Slices of whole grain bread (whole wheat, multigrain, or sprouted grain)
- Nut butter (almond butter, peanut butter, cashew butter, etc.)
- Optional toppings: sliced bananas, berries, chia seeds, honey, or cinnamon

Instructions:

1. Toast the slices of whole grain bread until golden brown and crispy.
2. Spread a generous layer of nut butter onto each slice of toast.
3. Top with sliced bananas, berries, chia seeds, a drizzle of honey, or a sprinkle of cinnamon if desired.
4. Serve immediately as a protein-packed breakfast or snack that's both delicious and nutritious.

2. Veggie-loaded Toasts:
Ingredients:

- Slices of bread (whole grain, sourdough, or rye)
- Hummus (store-bought or homemade)
- Assorted fresh vegetables (sliced tomatoes, cucumbers, bell peppers, avocado, shredded carrots, sprouts, etc.)
- Seeds (sunflower seeds, pumpkin seeds, sesame seeds, etc.)
- Salt and pepper to taste

Instructions:

1. Toast the slices of bread until golden brown and crispy.

2. Spread a thick layer of hummus onto each slice of toast.
3. Arrange a variety of fresh vegetables on top of the hummus.
4. Sprinkle with seeds, salt, and pepper to taste.
5. Serve immediately as a nutritious and satisfying meal that's bursting with color and flavor.

3. Quinoa Toast Toppers:
Ingredients:

- Slices of whole grain bread (whole wheat, multigrain, or sprouted grain)
- Cooked quinoa
- Assorted vegetables (diced tomatoes, cucumber, red onion, bell peppers, etc.)
- Fresh herbs (parsley, cilantro, basil, etc.)
- Lemon juice
- Olive oil
- Salt and pepper to taste

Instructions:

1. Toast the slices of whole grain bread until golden brown and crispy.
2. In a bowl, combine cooked quinoa, diced vegetables, chopped fresh herbs, lemon juice, olive oil, salt, and pepper.
3. Mix well to combine.
4. Spoon the quinoa salad onto each slice of toast.
5. Serve immediately as a wholesome and filling dish that's packed with protein, fiber, and flavor.

4. Tofu Scramble Toast:
Ingredients:

- Slices of whole grain bread (whole wheat, multigrain, or

sprouted grain)
- Firm tofu, drained and crumbled
- Olive oil
- Onion, diced
- Bell pepper, diced
- Spinach or kale, chopped
- Turmeric
- Garlic powder
- Salt and pepper to taste
- Avocado, sliced (optional)

Instructions:

1. Toast the slices of whole grain bread until golden brown and crispy.
2. In a skillet, heat olive oil over medium heat.
3. Add diced onion and bell pepper to the skillet and sauté until softened.
4. Add crumbled tofu to the skillet and sprinkle with turmeric, garlic powder, salt, and pepper.
5. Cook, stirring occasionally, until the tofu is heated through and lightly browned.
6. Add chopped spinach or kale to the skillet and cook until wilted.
7. Spoon the tofu scramble onto each slice of toast.
8. Top with sliced avocado if desired.
9. Serve immediately as a delicious and satisfying plant-based breakfast or brunch option.

Chapter 7: Seafood Sensations on Toast

1. Crab Toast:
Ingredients:

- Slices of bread (baguette, sourdough, or brioche)
- Lump crab meat
- Mayonnaise
- Lemon juice
- Fresh dill, chopped
- Salt and pepper to taste
- Lemon wedges for serving

Instructions

1. Toast the slices of bread until golden brown and crispy.
2. In a bowl, mix together lump crab meat, mayonnaise, lemon juice, chopped fresh dill, salt, and pepper until well combined.
3. Spread a generous portion of the creamy crab salad onto each slice of toast.
4. Squeeze a lemon wedge over each crab toast just before serving.
5. Serve immediately as a taste of the coast that's both luxurious and refreshing.

2. Tuna Melt:
Ingredients:

- Slices of bread (whole wheat, rye, or white)
- Canned tuna, drained
- Mayonnaise
- Dijon mustard
- Celery, finely chopped
- Red onion, finely chopped

- Shredded cheddar cheese
- Salt and pepper to taste

Instructions:

1. Toast the slices of bread until golden brown and crispy.
2. In a bowl, mix together canned tuna, mayonnaise, Dijon mustard, chopped celery, chopped red onion, salt, and pepper until well combined.
3. Spread the tuna salad mixture evenly onto each slice of toast.
4. Sprinkle shredded cheddar cheese over the tuna salad.
5. Place the tuna melt sandwiches under the broiler for 2-3 minutes, or until the cheese is melted and bubbly.
6. Remove from the oven and let cool slightly before serving.
7. Serve hot and enjoy this comforting and satisfying meal.

3. Shrimp Bruschetta:
Ingredients:

- Baguette, sliced into rounds
- Shrimp, peeled and deveined
- Olive oil
- Garlic cloves, minced
- Fresh herbs (parsley, basil, or thyme), chopped
- Salt and pepper to taste
- Lemon wedges for serving

Instructions:

1. Preheat the oven to 375°F (190°C).
2. Place the baguette slices on a baking sheet and toast them in the preheated oven for 5-7 minutes, or until lightly golden and crisp.
3. In a skillet, heat olive oil over medium heat.

4. Add minced garlic to the skillet and sauté until fragrant, about 1 minute.
5. Add shrimp to the skillet and cook until pink and opaque, about 2-3 minutes per side.
6. Season the shrimp with salt, pepper, and chopped fresh herbs.
7. Place a cooked shrimp on top of each toasted baguette slice.
8. Drizzle with a bit of garlic-infused olive oil from the skillet.
9. Squeeze a lemon wedge over each shrimp bruschetta just before serving.
10. Serve immediately as an elegant appetizer that's sure to impress.

4. Smoked Salmon Toast:
Ingredients:

- Slices of bread (whole grain, pumpernickel, or bagel)
- Cream cheese
- Smoked salmon
- Capers
- Red onion, thinly sliced
- Fresh dill sprigs
- Lemon wedges for serving

Instructions:

1. Toast the slices of bread until golden brown and crispy.
2. Spread a thick layer of cream cheese onto each slice of toast.
3. Arrange slices of smoked salmon on top of the cream cheese.
4. Sprinkle capers and thinly sliced red onion over the smoked salmon.
5. Garnish with fresh dill sprigs.
6. Serve with lemon wedges on the side for squeezing over the smoked salmon toast just before eating.
7. Serve immediately as a classic brunch favorite that's elegant and

delicious.

Chapter 8: Global Toast Inspirations

1. Indian Masala Toast:
Ingredients:

- Slices of bread (white, wheat, or multigrain)
- Potatoes, boiled and mashed
- Onion, finely chopped
- Green chilies, finely chopped
- Cilantro, chopped
- Chaat masala
- Salt to taste
- Green chutney
- Sev (crunchy chickpea noodles)
- Butter or ghee for toasting

Instructions:

1. In a bowl, mix together mashed potatoes, chopped onion, green chilies, cilantro, chaat masala, and salt to taste.
2. Spread a thick layer of the potato mixture onto each slice of bread.
3. Spread a layer of green chutney over the potato mixture.
4. Heat a skillet or griddle over medium heat and add a bit of butter or ghee.
5. Toast the bread slices on the skillet until golden brown and crispy on both sides.
6. Remove from the skillet and sprinkle crunchy sev over the top.
7. Serve hot as a flavorful and spicy Indian snack.

2. Japanese Tamago Sando:
Ingredients:

- Slices of Japanese milk bread or sandwich bread
- Eggs
- Japanese mayonnaise
- Soy sauce
- Sugar
- Salt and pepper to taste
- Optional: sliced cucumber or lettuce for extra crunch

Instructions:

1. In a bowl, whisk together eggs, Japanese mayonnaise, soy sauce, sugar, salt, and pepper until well combined.
2. Heat a non-stick skillet over medium heat and pour the egg mixture into the skillet.
3. Cook the egg mixture, stirring gently, until it forms a soft, fluffy omelette.
4. Remove the omelette from the skillet and let it cool slightly.
5. Place the omelette between two slices of lightly toasted bread.
6. If desired, add sliced cucumber or lettuce for extra crunch.
7. Cut the sandwich into halves or quarters and serve immediately as a sweet and savory Japanese treat.

3. Korean Kimchi Toast:
Ingredients:

- Slices of bread (whole wheat, sourdough, or rye)
- Kimchi
- Avocado, sliced
- Fried egg
- Soy sauce or gochujang (Korean chili paste) for drizzling (optional)
- Sesame seeds for garnish (optional)

Instructions:

1. Toast the slices of bread until golden brown and crispy.
2. Spread a layer of kimchi over each slice of toast.
3. Top with sliced avocado and a fried egg.
4. Drizzle with soy sauce or gochujang if desired.
5. Garnish with sesame seeds if desired.
6. Serve immediately as a fusion twist on traditional Korean flavors.

4. Middle Eastern Za'atar Toast:
Ingredients:

- Slices of bread (pita bread, naan, or baguette)
- Olive oil
- Za'atar spice blend
- Optional: Labneh (strained yogurt) or hummus for spreading

Instructions:

1. Preheat the oven to 375°F (190°C).
2. Brush each slice of bread with olive oil on both sides.
3. Sprinkle za'atar spice blend generously over each bread slice.
4. Place the bread slices on a baking sheet and bake in the preheated oven for 8-10 minutes, or until golden brown and crispy.
5. Remove from the oven and let cool slightly.
6. Serve as is or spread with labneh or hummus for added creaminess.
7. Enjoy this fragrant and savory Middle Eastern snack.

Chapter 9: Brunch Specialties

1. Eggs Benedict on Toast:
Ingredients:

- English muffins, split and toasted
- Eggs (for poaching)
- Canadian bacon or ham slices
- Hollandaise sauce (homemade or store-bought)
- Fresh chives or parsley for garnish (optional)

Instructions:

1. Toast the English muffin halves until lightly golden brown.
2. While the muffins are toasting, poach the eggs until the whites are set but the yolks are still runny.
3. Place a slice of Canadian bacon or ham on each toasted muffin half.
4. Carefully place a poached egg on top of each bacon/ham slice.
5. Spoon hollandaise sauce generously over the eggs.
6. Garnish with fresh chives or parsley if desired.
7. Serve immediately as a classic and indulgent brunch dish.

2. Breakfast BLT:
Ingredients:

- Slices of bread (white, wheat, or sourdough), toasted
- Crispy bacon slices
- Lettuce leaves
- Sliced tomatoes
- Mayonnaise
- Salt and pepper to taste

Instructions:

1. Toast the slices of bread until golden brown and crispy.
2. Spread mayonnaise on one side of each toasted bread slice.
3. Layer crispy bacon, lettuce leaves, and sliced tomatoes on one bread slice.
4. Season with salt and pepper to taste.
5. Top with the second bread slice, mayonnaise side down.
6. Slice the sandwich in half diagonally and serve immediately as a satisfying morning meal.

3. Huevos Rancheros Toast:
Ingredients:

- Slices of bread (whole grain, sourdough, or cornbread), toasted
- Refried beans
- Fried eggs
- Salsa
- Avocado slices
- Fresh cilantro leaves
- Lime wedges (optional)

Instructions:

1. Spread a layer of refried beans onto each slice of toasted bread.
2. Top with a fried egg.
3. Spoon salsa over the eggs.
4. Add avocado slices on top.
5. Garnish with fresh cilantro leaves.
6. Serve with lime wedges on the side if desired.
7. Serve immediately as a hearty and flavorful brunch option.

4. Croissant French Toast:
Ingredients:

- Croissants, sliced in half horizontally
- Eggs
- Milk or cream
- Vanilla extract
- Butter for cooking
- Maple syrup for serving

Instructions:

1. In a shallow bowl, whisk together eggs, milk or cream, and vanilla extract until well combined.
2. Dip each croissant half into the egg mixture, ensuring it's evenly coated on both sides.
3. Heat butter in a skillet over medium heat.
4. Place the soaked croissant halves in the skillet and cook until golden brown and crispy on both sides.
5. Remove from the skillet and serve immediately with maple syrup drizzled on top.
6. Enjoy this decadent brunch treat!

Chapter 10: Toasted Bread Bites for Entertaining

1. Toasted Bread Canapés:
Ingredients:

- Baguette or small bread slices, toasted
- Assorted savory spreads (such as cream cheese, pesto, tapenade, hummus)
- Various cheeses (such as brie, goat cheese, blue cheese)
- Garnishes (such as sliced olives, cherry tomatoes, fresh herbs, caramelized onions)

Instructions:

1. Cut the toasted bread into bite-sized pieces.
2. Spread each bread piece with a different savory spread.
3. Top with a variety of cheeses and garnishes.
4. Arrange the canapés on a serving platter and serve immediately as elegant party appetizers.

2. Antipasto Toast Skewers:
Ingredients:

- Toasted bread cubes
- Italian meats (such as salami, prosciutto, mortadella)
- Cheeses (such as mozzarella balls, provolone, Parmesan)
- Marinated vegetables (such as cherry tomatoes, artichoke hearts, roasted peppers)
- Olives
- Wooden skewers

Instructions:

1. Thread toasted bread cubes, Italian meats, cheeses, marinated vegetables, and olives onto wooden skewers in any combination you like.
2. Arrange the skewers on a platter and serve immediately as a colorful and delicious party snack.

3. Toasted Bread Bruschetta Bar:
Ingredients:

- Toasted bread slices (baguette, ciabatta, or sourdough)
- Assorted toppings (such as diced tomatoes, fresh basil, sliced mozzarella, marinated artichokes, roasted garlic, pesto, balsamic glaze)
- Spreads (such as ricotta cheese, goat cheese, hummus)
- Olive oil, for drizzling

Instructions:

1. Set up a DIY station with toasted bread slices and bowls of assorted toppings, spreads, and sauces.
2. Encourage guests to create their own bruschetta masterpieces by topping the toasted bread slices with their favorite combinations.
3. Provide olive oil for drizzling over the bruschetta creations.
4. Allow guests to enjoy their custom-made bruschetta immediately.

4. Toasted Bread Crostini Platter:
Ingredients:

- Assorted toasted bread slices (baguette, French bread, whole grain)

- Various toppings (such as sliced cured meats, cheeses, fruits, nuts, herbs)
- Spreads (such as fig jam, olive tapenade, honey mustard)
- Olive oil, for drizzling

Instructions:

1. Arrange the toasted bread slices on a large platter.
2. Top each slice with a different combination of toppings, spreads, and herbs.
3. Drizzle olive oil over the crostini platter for added flavor.
4. Serve the crostini platter as a stunning appetizer display for guests to enjoy.

Chapter 11: Creative Vegan Toast Ideas

1. Vegan Caprese Toast:
Ingredients:

- Slices of bread (sourdough, whole grain, or ciabatta), toasted
- Fresh tomatoes, sliced
- Fresh basil leaves
- Dairy-free mozzarella cheese, sliced or shredded
- Balsamic glaze (optional)
- Salt and pepper to taste

Instructions:

1. Place the toasted bread slices on a serving plate.
2. Arrange slices of fresh tomato on top of each toast.
3. Top each tomato slice with a fresh basil leaf.
4. Add slices or shredded dairy-free mozzarella cheese on top.
5. Drizzle with balsamic glaze if desired.
6. Season with salt and pepper to taste.
7. Serve immediately as a plant-based twist on the classic Italian Caprese salad.

2. Chickpea Salad Toast:
Ingredients:

- Slices of bread (whole grain, sourdough, or multigrain), toasted
- Ripe avocado, mashed
- Chickpeas, drained and rinsed
- Red onion, finely chopped
- Cherry tomatoes, halved
- Cucumber, diced
- Fresh parsley or cilantro, chopped

- Lemon juice
- Olive oil
- Salt and pepper to taste

Instructions:

1. Spread mashed avocado onto each slice of toasted bread.
2. In a bowl, combine chickpeas, red onion, cherry tomatoes, cucumber, and fresh herbs.
3. Drizzle with lemon juice and olive oil, and season with salt and pepper.
4. Spoon the chickpea salad mixture on top of the mashed avocado.
5. Serve immediately as a flavorful and satisfying vegan lunch option.

3. Vegan "Egg" Salad Toast:
Ingredients:

- Slices of bread (whole grain, rye, or gluten-free), toasted
- Firm tofu, drained and crumbled
- Vegan mayonnaise
- Dijon mustard
- Turmeric
- Chopped chives
- Salt and pepper to taste
- Lettuce leaves or sprouts (optional)

Instructions:

1. In a bowl, mix together crumbled tofu, vegan mayonnaise, Dijon mustard, turmeric, chopped chives, salt, and pepper until well combined.
2. Spread the tofu "egg" salad onto each slice of toasted bread.

3. Add lettuce leaves or sprouts on top if desired.
4. Serve immediately as a cruelty-free alternative to traditional egg salad sandwiches.

4. Vegan BBQ Jackfruit Toast:
Ingredients:

- Slices of bread (ciabatta, French bread, or sandwich bread), toasted
- BBQ jackfruit (either homemade or store-bought)
- Vegan coleslaw
- Pickles, sliced
- BBQ sauce
- Fresh cilantro, chopped (optional)

Instructions:

1. Spread BBQ jackfruit onto each slice of toasted bread.
2. Top with vegan coleslaw and sliced pickles.
3. Drizzle with extra BBQ sauce if desired.
4. Garnish with fresh chopped cilantro if desired.
5. Serve immediately as a hearty and flavorful vegan sandwich option.

Chapter 12: Toasted Bread Dessert Innovations

1. Bread and Nutella S'mores:
Ingredients:

- Slices of bread (white, wheat, or brioche), toasted
- Nutella (or any chocolate hazelnut spread)
- Marshmallows

Instructions:

1. Spread Nutella generously onto each slice of toasted bread.
2. Place marshmallows on top of the Nutella layer.
3. Use a kitchen torch or broiler to toast the marshmallows until golden and gooey.
4. Serve immediately as a decadent twist on the classic campfire treat.

2. Toasted Bread Banoffee Pie:
Ingredients:

- Slices of bread (white, wheat, or brioche), toasted
- Caramel sauce (homemade or store-bought)
- Sliced bananas
- Whipped cream
- Chocolate shavings or cocoa powder

Instructions:

1. Layer toasted bread slices with caramel sauce, sliced bananas, and whipped cream in a serving dish or individual glasses.

2. Repeat the layers until the dish or glasses are filled.
3. Sprinkle chocolate shavings or cocoa powder on top for garnish.
4. Refrigerate for at least 1 hour before serving to allow the flavors to meld together.
5. Serve chilled as a delicious and easy no-bake dessert option.

3. Toasted Bread Berry Parfait:
Ingredients:

- Slices of bread (whole grain, sourdough, or cinnamon raisin), toasted and cubed
- Greek yogurt (or dairy-free yogurt)
- Mixed berries (such as strawberries, blueberries, raspberries)
- Honey or maple syrup (optional)
- Granola (optional)

Instructions:

1. In serving glasses or bowls, layer toasted bread cubes with Greek yogurt and mixed berries.
2. Drizzle each layer with honey or maple syrup if desired.
3. Repeat the layers until the glasses or bowls are filled, ending with a layer of mixed berries on top.
4. Optionally, sprinkle granola on top for added crunch.
5. Serve immediately as a refreshing and satisfying dessert parfait.

4. Toasted Bread Bread Pudding Cups:
Ingredients:

- Slices of bread (stale or toasted), cubed
- Raisins or dried fruit (optional)
- Eggs

- Milk or dairy-free milk
- Sugar
- Vanilla extract
- Cinnamon
- Nutmeg
- Butter or cooking spray, for greasing

Instructions:

1. Preheat the oven to 350°F (175°C) and grease individual ramekins or muffin tins with butter or cooking spray.
2. In a bowl, whisk together eggs, milk, sugar, vanilla extract, cinnamon, and nutmeg until well combined.
3. Add the cubed bread and raisins or dried fruit to the egg mixture and stir until the bread is evenly coated.
4. Divide the bread pudding mixture evenly among the prepared ramekins or muffin tins.
5. Bake in the preheated oven for 20-25 minutes, or until the bread pudding is set and golden brown on top.
6. Remove from the oven and let cool slightly before serving.
7. Serve the bread pudding cups warm as a comforting and satisfying dessert.

Chapter 13: Toasted Bread for Soup and Salad

1. Toasted Bread Panzanella Salad:
Ingredients:

- Slices of bread (rustic Italian bread, ciabatta, or baguette), cubed and toasted
- Ripe tomatoes, diced
- Cucumber, diced
- Red onion, thinly sliced
- Fresh basil leaves, torn
- Balsamic vinegar
- Extra virgin olive oil
- Salt and pepper to taste

Instructions:

1. In a large bowl, combine the toasted bread cubes, diced tomatoes, diced cucumber, thinly sliced red onion, and torn basil leaves.
2. Drizzle with balsamic vinegar and extra virgin olive oil.
3. Season with salt and pepper to taste.
4. Toss gently to coat all the ingredients evenly.
5. Let the salad sit for about 10 minutes to allow the flavors to meld together.
6. Serve chilled or at room temperature as a refreshing summer dish.

2. Toasted Bread Croutons:
Ingredients:

- Slices of bread (French baguette, sourdough, or whole wheat), cubed
- Olive oil
- Garlic powder
- Italian seasoning (optional)
- Salt and pepper to taste

Instructions:

1. Preheat the oven to 375°F (190°C) and line a baking sheet with parchment paper.
2. In a large bowl, toss the bread cubes with olive oil, garlic powder, Italian seasoning (if using), salt, and pepper until evenly coated.
3. Spread the bread cubes in a single layer on the prepared baking sheet.
4. Bake in the preheated oven for 10-15 minutes, or until the croutons are golden brown and crispy, tossing halfway through.
5. Remove from the oven and let cool completely before using.
6. Store any leftover croutons in an airtight container at room temperature for up to 1 week.

3. Toasted Bread Gazpacho Shooters:
Ingredients:

- Gazpacho soup (homemade or store-bought), chilled
- Toasted bread croutons
- Fresh herbs (such as parsley, cilantro, or basil) for garnish

Instructions:

1. Ladle chilled gazpacho soup into small shot glasses or mini cups.
2. Garnish each shooter with a few toasted bread croutons.

3. Sprinkle with fresh herbs for added flavor and color.
4. Serve immediately as a refreshing appetizer or amuse-bouche at your next gathering.

Chapter 14: Toasted Bread for Special Diets

1. Gluten-Free Toasted Bread Options:
Ingredients:

- Gluten-free bread slices (store-bought or homemade)

Instructions:

1. Preheat your toaster or oven to the desired temperature for toasting gluten-free bread.
2. Place the gluten-free bread slices into the toaster or on a baking sheet if using the oven.
3. Toast the bread slices until they are golden brown and crispy, making sure not to burn them.
4. Once toasted, remove the bread slices from the toaster or oven and allow them to cool slightly before serving.
5. Enjoy your gluten-free toasted bread with your favorite toppings, spreads, or as a side with soups and salads.

Tips for Toasting Gluten-Free Bread:

- Gluten-free bread tends to be more delicate and may require a shorter toasting time than regular bread to avoid becoming too dry or crumbly.
- Check the texture of the bread frequently while toasting to prevent overcooking.
- If using a toaster, consider using a lower setting or toasting the bread twice on a lighter setting to achieve optimal crispiness without burning.

2. Keto-Friendly Toasted Bread Alternatives:

Almond Flour Toasted Bread:
Ingredients:

- 1 cup almond flour
- 2 tablespoons coconut flour
- 1 teaspoon baking powder
- 1/4 teaspoon salt
- 2 large eggs
- 1/4 cup unsweetened almond milk
- 2 tablespoons melted coconut oil

Instructions:

1. Preheat your oven to 350°F (175°C) and line a baking sheet with parchment paper.
2. In a mixing bowl, whisk together almond flour, coconut flour, baking powder, and salt.
3. In a separate bowl, beat the eggs and then stir in almond milk and melted coconut oil.
4. Gradually add the wet ingredients to the dry ingredients and mix until well combined.
5. Pour the batter onto the prepared baking sheet and spread it out evenly.
6. Bake for 15-20 minutes, or until the bread is golden brown and cooked through.
7. Once baked, remove from the oven and let it cool slightly before slicing.
8. Toast the slices of almond flour bread in a toaster or toaster oven until crispy and golden brown.
9. Serve warm with your favorite toppings or as a side dish.

3. Paleo Toasted Bread Recipes:
Seed-Based Paleo Bread:

Ingredients:

- 1 cup almond flour
- 1/4 cup flaxseed meal
- 1/4 cup pumpkin seeds
- 1/4 cup sunflower seeds
- 1/4 cup chia seeds
- 1/4 cup coconut oil, melted
- 3 large eggs
- 1 teaspoon baking soda
- 1 tablespoon apple cider vinegar
- Pinch of salt

Instructions:

1. Preheat your oven to 350°F (175°C) and line a loaf pan with parchment paper.
2. In a food processor, pulse together almond flour, flaxseed meal, pumpkin seeds, sunflower seeds, and chia seeds until finely ground.
3. In a mixing bowl, whisk together melted coconut oil, eggs, baking soda, apple cider vinegar, and salt.
4. Gradually add the dry ingredients to the wet ingredients and mix until a thick batter forms.
5. Pour the batter into the prepared loaf pan and smooth out the top.
6. Bake for 40-45 minutes, or until the bread is golden brown and firm to the touch.
7. Once baked, remove from the oven and let it cool in the pan for 10 minutes before transferring to a wire rack to cool completely.
8. Once cooled, slice the bread into desired thickness and toast in a toaster or toaster oven until crispy and golden brown.
9. Serve toasted seed-based paleo bread with your favorite

toppings or as a side with soups and salads.

Chapter 15: Toasted Bread Beverages and Cocktails

1. Bread Tea:
Ingredients:

- Toasted bread crusts or bread crumbs
- Water
- Cinnamon sticks
- Cardamom pods
- Honey or sugar (optional, to taste)

Instructions:

1. In a saucepan, bring water to a boil.
2. Add toasted bread crusts or bread crumbs to the boiling water.
3. Reduce the heat to low and let the mixture simmer for about 10-15 minutes to infuse the flavors.
4. Add cinnamon sticks and cardamom pods to the saucepan and continue to simmer for another 5 minutes.
5. Remove the saucepan from the heat and strain the bread tea into cups.
6. Sweeten with honey or sugar if desired.
7. Serve hot and enjoy this unique and comforting beverage.

2. Bread-infused Cocktails:
Bread-Infused Bourbon:
Ingredients:

- Bourbon whiskey
- Slices of toasted bread (any variety)
- Mason jar or airtight container

Instructions:

1. Place toasted bread slices into a mason jar or airtight container.
2. Pour bourbon whiskey over the toasted bread until it's fully submerged.
3. Seal the jar tightly and let it sit at room temperature for 2-3 days to allow the flavors to infuse.
4. After infusing, strain the bourbon through a fine-mesh sieve or cheesecloth to remove the bread particles.
5. Transfer the infused bourbon back into a clean bottle for storage.
6. Use the bread-infused bourbon to make cocktails like Old Fashioneds or Manhattan for a unique twist.

Bread-Infused Vodka:
Ingredients:

- Vodka
- Slices of toasted bread (any variety)
- Mason jar or airtight container

Instructions:

1. Follow the same steps as above for the bread-infused bourbon, substituting vodka for bourbon.
2. Let the vodka and toasted bread infuse for 2-3 days at room

temperature.

3. Strain the infused vodka through a fine-mesh sieve or cheesecloth to remove any bread particles.
4. Store the bread-infused vodka in a clean bottle for future use.
5. Use the bread-infused vodka to create cocktails like Bloody Marys or vodka martinis for a distinctive flavor profile.

Chapter 16: Toasted Bread for Bruschetta Varieties

1. Fig and Goat Cheese Bruschetta:
Ingredients:

- Slices of bread (baguette or ciabatta), toasted
- Creamy goat cheese
- Fresh figs, sliced
- Honey
- Fresh thyme leaves

Instructions:

1. Spread a layer of creamy goat cheese onto each slice of toasted bread.
2. Arrange sliced figs on top of the goat cheese.
3. Drizzle honey over the figs.
4. Sprinkle fresh thyme leaves on top for garnish.
5. Serve immediately as a sweet and savory appetizer.

2. Prosciutto and Melon Bruschetta:
Ingredients:

- Slices of bread (French baguette or sourdough), toasted
- Thinly sliced prosciutto
- Melon balls (cantaloupe or honeydew)
- Balsamic glaze
- Fresh basil leaves for garnish

Instructions:

1. Place a slice of thinly sliced prosciutto on each slice of toasted

bread.
2. Top with melon balls.
3. Drizzle balsamic glaze over the bruschetta.
4. Garnish with fresh basil leaves.
5. Serve immediately as a refreshing and elegant starter.

3. Brie and Cranberry Bruschetta:
Ingredients:

- Slices of bread (baguette or ciabatta), toasted
- Brie cheese, sliced
- Cranberry sauce
- Fresh rosemary sprigs for garnish

Instructions:

1. Place a slice of brie cheese on each slice of toasted bread.
2. Spoon cranberry sauce over the brie.
3. Garnish with fresh rosemary sprigs.
4. Serve immediately as a festive and flavorful holiday appetizer.

4. Ricotta and Honey Bruschetta:
Ingredients:

- Slices of bread (whole grain or sourdough), toasted
- Ricotta cheese
- Honey
- Toasted pine nuts for garnish

Instructions:

1. Spread a layer of ricotta cheese onto each slice of toasted bread.
2. Drizzle honey over the ricotta.
3. Sprinkle toasted pine nuts on top for garnish.

4. Serve immediately as a simple yet delicious treat.

Chapter 17: Toasted Bread Bites for Tapas

1. Spanish Tomato Toast (Pan con Tomate):
Ingredients:

- Slices of bread (baguette or rustic country bread), toasted
- Ripe tomatoes, halved
- Garlic cloves, peeled
- Extra virgin olive oil
- Sea salt

Instructions:

1. Rub the toasted bread slices with the peeled garlic cloves.
2. Rub the cut side of the ripe tomatoes over the garlic-rubbed bread to impart flavor and moisture.
3. Drizzle extra virgin olive oil over the tomato-rubbed bread.
4. Sprinkle with sea salt.
5. Serve immediately as a classic Spanish tapa.

2. Chorizo and Manchego Toasts:
Ingredients:

- Slices of bread (baguette or ciabatta), toasted
- Thinly sliced chorizo sausage
- Shaved Manchego cheese
- Spicy aioli (mayonnaise mixed with minced garlic and a dash of hot sauce)

Instructions:

1. Top each slice of toasted bread with thinly sliced chorizo sausage.
2. Add a few shavings of Manchego cheese on top.

3. Dollop a small amount of spicy aioli on each toast.
4. Serve immediately as a flavorful bite-sized appetizer.

3. Spanish Tortilla Bites:
Ingredients:

- Slices of bread (baguette or rustic country bread), toasted and cut into squares
- Spanish tortilla (potato omelet), sliced into squares
- Roasted red peppers, sliced into strips
- Aioli (garlic mayonnaise)

Instructions:

- Place a slice of Spanish tortilla on top of each toasted bread square.
- Add a strip of roasted red pepper on top of the tortilla.
- Garnish with a dollop of aioli.
- Serve immediately as a traditional tapas dish.

4. Patatas Bravas Toasts:
Ingredients:

- Slices of bread (baguette or ciabatta), toasted
- Diced potatoes, roasted until crispy
- Spicy tomato sauce
- Garlic aioli

Instructions:

1. Top each slice of toasted bread with a spoonful of crispy diced potatoes.
2. Drizzle with spicy tomato sauce.
3. Garnish with a dollop of garlic aioli.

4. Serve immediately as a satisfying and flavorful tapas option.

Chapter 18: Toasted Bread for Party Platters

1. Mediterranean Toasted Bread Platter:
Ingredients:

- Assorted toasted bread slices (baguette, pita, or ciabatta)
- Hummus
- Tzatziki sauce
- Marinated olives
- Roasted vegetables (such as bell peppers, zucchini, and eggplant)
- Feta cheese, crumbled
- Fresh herbs (such as parsley or dill), for garnish
- Extra virgin olive oil, for drizzling
- Lemon wedges, for serving

Instructions:

1. Arrange the assorted toasted bread slices on a large platter.
2. Place bowls of hummus and tzatziki sauce on the platter.
3. Scatter marinated olives, roasted vegetables, and crumbled feta cheese around the bread slices.
4. Garnish with fresh herbs and drizzle extra virgin olive oil over the platter.
5. Serve with lemon wedges on the side for squeezing over the toppings.

2. Charcuterie Toasted Bread Board:
Ingredients:

- Assorted toasted bread slices (baguette, sourdough, or rye)
- Cured meats (such as prosciutto, salami, and chorizo)
- Artisan cheeses (such as aged cheddar, brie, and blue cheese)
- Pickles (such as cornichons and pickled onions)
- Mustards (such as Dijon and whole grain)
- Fruit preserves (such as fig jam and apricot preserves)
- Fresh fruits (such as grapes and apple slices)
- Nuts (such as almonds and walnuts)

Instructions:

1. Arrange the assorted toasted bread slices on a large wooden board or platter.
2. Arrange the cured meats and artisan cheeses around the bread slices.
3. Place small bowls of pickles, mustards, and fruit preserves on the board.
4. Scatter fresh fruits and nuts around the board for garnish.
5. Serve as a stunning charcuterie display for your party guests to enjoy.

3. Vegetarian Toasted Bread Grazing Platter:
Ingredients:

- Assorted toasted bread rounds (baguette, whole grain, or gluten-free)
- Vegetarian spreads and dips (such as hummus, baba ganoush, and spinach artichoke dip)
- Crudites (such as carrot sticks, cucumber slices, and bell pepper strips)
- Nuts (such as almonds and cashews)

- Dried fruits (such as apricots and figs)
- Fresh herbs (such as parsley and cilantro), for garnish

Instructions:

1. Arrange the assorted toasted bread rounds on a large platter.
2. Place bowls of vegetarian spreads and dips on the platter.
3. Arrange crudites, nuts, and dried fruits around the bread rounds.
4. Garnish with fresh herbs for added color and flavor.
5. Serve as a crowd-pleasing vegetarian appetizer option at your next gathering.

4. Seafood Toasted Bread Sampler:
Ingredients:

- Assorted toasted bread slices (baguette or sourdough)
- Smoked salmon
- Shrimp cocktail
- Crab salad
- Tuna tartare
- Lemon wedges
- Fresh dill, for garnish

Instructions:

1. Arrange the assorted toasted bread slices on a large platter.
2. Place small piles of smoked salmon, shrimp cocktail, crab salad, and tuna tartare on the platter, leaving space between each pile.
3. Garnish with lemon wedges and fresh dill.
4. Serve as an elegant seafood platter for your party guests to enjoy.

Chapter 19: Toasted Bread Around the World

1. Turkish Kofta Toasts:
  Ingredients:

- Slices of bread (pita or flatbread), toasted
- Grilled lamb kofta (spiced meatballs)
- Tzatziki sauce
- Chopped fresh herbs (such as parsley or mint)
- Lemon wedges, for serving

Instructions:

1. Place a grilled lamb kofta on each slice of toasted bread.
2. Drizzle tzatziki sauce over the kofta.
3. Sprinkle with chopped fresh herbs.
4. Serve with lemon wedges on the side for squeezing over the toasts.
5. Enjoy this flavorful Turkish-inspired snack.

2. Dutch Hagelslag Toast:
Ingredients:

- Slices of bread (white or whole wheat), toasted
- Butter
- Chocolate sprinkles (hagelslag)

Instructions:

1. Spread butter generously on each slice of toasted bread while it's still warm.

2. Sprinkle colorful chocolate sprinkles (hagelslag) over the buttered toast.
3. Serve immediately as a sweet and indulgent Dutch treat.

3. Brazilian Pão de Queijo Toast:
Ingredients:

- Slices of bread (French or Italian), toasted
- Pão de queijo (cheese bread) dough
- Grated cheese (such as Parmesan or Pecorino Romano)
- Fresh parsley, chopped (optional)

Instructions:

1. Preheat the oven to 375°F (190°C) and line a baking sheet with parchment paper.
2. Place slices of toasted bread on the prepared baking sheet.
3. Flatten small portions of pão de queijo dough and place them on top of the toasted bread slices.
4. Sprinkle grated cheese over the pão de queijo dough.
5. Bake in the preheated oven for 10-12 minutes, or until the cheese is melted and bubbly, and the bread is golden brown.
6. Garnish with chopped fresh parsley, if desired.
7. Serve warm as a cheesy and delicious Brazilian snack.

4. Thai Peanut Toasts:
Ingredients:

- Slices of bread (baguette or sandwich bread), toasted
- Spicy peanut sauce
- Shredded chicken, cooked
- Cucumber slices

- Fresh cilantro leaves

Instructions:

1. Spread spicy peanut sauce generously on each slice of toasted bread.
2. Top with shredded chicken and cucumber slices.
3. Garnish with fresh cilantro leaves.
4. Serve immediately as a flavorful Thai-inspired snack.

Chapter 20: Toasted Bread for Kids and Families

1. Pizza Toast Faces:
Ingredients:

- Slices of bread (white or whole wheat), toasted
- Pizza sauce
- Shredded mozzarella cheese
- Assorted toppings (such as pepperoni slices, diced bell peppers, sliced olives, and cherry tomatoes)

Instructions:

1. Preheat the oven to 375°F (190°C).
2. Spread pizza sauce on each slice of toasted bread.
3. Sprinkle shredded mozzarella cheese over the sauce.
4. Decorate each pizza toast with assorted toppings to create fun and customizable pizza faces.
5. Place the pizza toasts on a baking sheet and bake in the preheated oven for 8-10 minutes, or until the cheese is melted and bubbly.
6. Serve hot and enjoy these playful pizza faces with your family.

2. Teddy Bear Toasts:
Ingredients:

- Slices of bread (whole wheat or multigrain), toasted
- Peanut butter
- Banana slices
- Raisins

Instructions:

1. Use a teddy bear-shaped cookie cutter to cut out teddy bear shapes from the toasted bread slices.
2. Spread peanut butter on each teddy bear toast.
3. Place banana slices on top to create the ears and snout of the teddy bear.
4. Use raisins to make the eyes, nose, and mouth of the teddy bear.
5. Serve these adorable teddy bear toasts as a cute and playful snack for kids.

3. Sandwich Sushi Rolls:
Ingredients:

- Slices of bread (white or whole wheat), toasted
- Cream cheese
- Assorted sandwich fillings (such as deli meat, cheese slices, lettuce, and cucumber)
- Optional: condiments like mustard or mayonnaise

Instructions:

1. Flatten each slice of toasted bread with a rolling pin.
2. Spread cream cheese evenly over the flattened bread slices.
3. Place your desired sandwich fillings along one edge of each bread slice.
4. Roll up the bread slices tightly, starting from the edge with the fillings.
5. Use a sharp knife to slice each roll into bite-sized pieces, like sushi rolls.
6. Serve these sandwich sushi rolls as a fun and kid-friendly lunch or snack option.

4. Fairy Bread:
Ingredients:

- Slices of bread (white or whole wheat), toasted
- Butter
- Colorful sprinkles

Instructions:

1. Spread butter generously over each slice of toasted bread.
2. Pour colorful sprinkles onto a plate.
3. Place the buttered side of the bread slices onto the plate of sprinkles, pressing down gently to adhere the sprinkles to the bread.
4. Lift the fairy bread slices carefully and shake off any excess sprinkles.
5. Serve these whimsical and nostalgic fairy bread slices as a fun treat loved by kids of all ages.

❖ Conclusion:

Toasted Bread Beyond Boundaries:
Throughout this journey, we've explored the boundless culinary world of toasted bread. From classic recipes to innovative creations inspired by cuisines from around the globe, toasted bread has proven to be a versatile canvas for creativity and flavor exploration. Whether it's a simple snack or an elaborate party platter, toasted bread has a place in every kitchen and every occasion.

Tips and Tricks:
As you continue to experiment with toasted bread in your own kitchen, here are some final words of wisdom and tips to help you master the art of toasting bread:

1. Choose the Right Bread: Different types of bread offer different textures and flavors when toasted. Experiment with various bread varieties, from crusty baguettes to hearty whole grain loaves, to find the perfect match for your recipe.

2. Control the Heat: Whether you're using a toaster, oven, or stovetop, controlling the heat is essential for achieving the perfect toast. Keep an eye on your bread to prevent burning, and adjust the cooking time and temperature as needed.

3. Get Creative with Toppings: Don't be afraid to think outside the box when it comes to topping your toasted bread. Explore a wide range of sweet and savory ingredients to create unique flavor combinations and stunning presentations.

4. Embrace Versatility: Toasted bread can be enjoyed in countless ways, from simple snacks to elaborate meals. Let your imagination run wild and experiment with different recipes and techniques to discover new and exciting ways to enjoy toasted bread.

5. Share the Joy: Food has a special way of bringing people

together, and toasted bread is no exception. Whether you're cooking for family, friends, or yourself, sharing your love for toasted bread and the delicious creations you've made is a wonderful way to spread joy and happiness.

With these tips and tricks in mind, may your culinary adventures with toasted bread continue to delight and inspire. Happy toasting!